Some Gods Don't Need Saints

poems by

Mary Catherine Harper

Finishing Line Press
Georgetown, Kentucky

Some Gods Don't Need Saints

Copyright © 2016 by Mary Catherine Harper
ISBN 978-1-944899-42-4 First Edition
All rights reserved under International and Pan-American Copyright Conventions. No part of this book may be reproduced in any manner whatsoever without written permission from the publisher, except in the case of brief quotations embodied in critical articles and reviews.

Editor: Christen Kincaid

Cover Art: Kathy Funderburg, "Patience"

Author Photo: Kristi Jo Leaders

Cover Design: Amy K. Drees

Printed in the USA on acid-free paper.
Order online: www.finishinglinepress.com
also available on amazon.com

Author inquiries and mail orders:
Finishing Line Press
P. O. Box 1626
Georgetown, Kentucky 40324
U. S. A.

Table of Contents

The Spider Talks to Her Creation 1

Joan of Arc 2

Tiresias among the Sycamores 3

The Little Idol of the House 5

Before Adam Was Cast 7

The Patron Saint of Ruin 9

Columbine and Citrus 10

Pandora's Box 11

To Cain and Abel 12

Esau without a Face 13

Salsify 14

Piss on Saints 16

Reading Tarot 17

Heavy as a Wife's Body 18

Some Gods Don't Need Saints 19

Martyr's End 20

Of Spiders 21

Ts'its'tsi'nako 22

Disabled Gods 23

*To Dawn, Marian, and Jerri,
for all they know and share*

The Spider Talks to Her Creation

*In Keresan mythology Ts'its'tsi'nako spins stories
out of her body, and her stories are the universe.*

I settle my heavy body near the foundation
of your house
and thread me close to the dandelion star
you intend to kill
when the weather dries up
and the wind ends.

How to undo
your obsession with classifying green things
into crab or fruit,
weed or grass,
how to undo
the web, pull back time into my spinneret.

I wait for your foundation to crumble enough
to crack
into your basement
to thread some wild fragile leavings there
across the bottom
of your world.

Joan of Arc

What if it had been her intention
all along,
a competition with Archangel
Michael,
a brash move on the narrow
chessboard
of a world of mud and blood,
the winner
to choose where to plant God's
heart.

What if the Maid of Orléans was
no maid,
but the resolute lover of a land
of men,
experienced in the ways of earthy
sex,
so firm in her plan to seduce
love
out of an untouchable and distant
God
that she sinned happily, our Patron
of Willfulness.

Tiresias among the Sycamores

Remember how it happened,
the inscrutable plan
against your singular direction?

When the sycamores found
blood between your legs
on that first day as a woman,
they took pity,
knowing the old story.

But you refused the dance
of broad leaves,
being disturbed enough having
to navigate the world in two
human bodies.

You still hear them call,
sycamore to sister,
knowing these sky-rubbing trees
speak in tongues beyond
the scrape they make of sky.

Do you know why
they bare their sage and birch
white arms longer
than other winter-loving trees?

Past the coziness
of hibernating dreams,
until summer's first heat,
they wait for you.

They dream your memory
of a man coming in
and a woman going out,
you bearing both.

They, the heart of green wood
that would take you for
their own
and dance the world
to full-blooming ambiguity
if you only would.

The Little Idol of the House

The little idol of the house
crouches in the corner
and remembers how the family
once rubbed its belly with oil
to keep its heart and bones
from cracking out of jet wood,
its back and buttocks still
bearing the whorl
of the mother's index finger
and the middle finger's tented arch
long after she vanished from life.

The little idol of the house
smells the hundred
pounds of garlic
the father is running through
a hand grinder to mix with
the cuts of pork meant
to be turned into sausage
in the next room,
and wishes its interrogation
of destiny had come
much earlier in its protracted life,
or at least before it thought
to tantalize the wood carver
with that felicitous fate line
blooming through the bark
of the tree where it once lived.

The little idol of the house
cringes at the atheism that men
and their sons sometimes develop,
imagines being butchered
like an animal by the man
who grows squat
and sits cross-legged
at the end of the day
swatting flies near the god
he's forgotten
to feed and dust.

Before Adam Was Cast

What of the human being
with a myth on her chest?

You who have no tongue,
only wool and loom
to tell the horror story
of your brother-in-law
dragging you through
the woods to the secret
shed of his adultery

What happened the day
before Tereus forced you?

You who have no land,
only a mother-in-law
you've fallen in love with
so deeply you'll follow
anywhere, everywhere
or nowhere with her people
still calling you "outsider"

What brought contentment
before Naomi walked in?

You the first, left behind,
with only a weedy garden
to keep your willful self
company, your husband
and his second wife
being forced out for
the rebellion you started

What were you thinking
before Adam was cast?

The Patron Saint of Ruin

Lilith was born with deep turquoise eyes
that tinted her sight like a gel on a camera
so when she spied on God's surgery
and saw the bloody rib from Adam's side,
it was the dirty hue of bruise before it stirred
and gulped in air, breathing by its own will.

Hers is a story both true and phantasmagoric,
a gurgle of episodes that would take a teller
longer to relate than the time that wheat uses
to turn itself from grass to blue-green to rust,
so I offer this mere scrap of extant testimony,
the fragment of her speech to Eve before
withdrawing to the bark of a nearby tree:

I was destined for legend before my birth,
the myth of woman's free dance and song
twisted into rag and thrown to the midden.
But I'm still here, the patron saint of ruin.
I dust the belly of a snake for my pleasure.
I drip from the green pears in your orchard,
draining them of juice before they ripen.
I crumble into grains of sand on your beach
and worm myself between your buttocks.
I cloud your eye with smoke from your fire.
I ride a dragonfly's back to tease your sex.
I pin my tongue to your baby's breath.

Columbine and Citrus

I

I return to the garden
through the fence and gate I built
and slammed behind your back
as your wife stumbled
to the dust, pregnant,
and I kick the fence.

II

I return to the garden
overgrown with columbine and citrus
and a bird species you forgot to name
and send to the zoo
in the city you built,
and I smile at my bird.

III

I return to the garden
where your first mate still walks
among her Lily of the Valley
drunk on the floral scent,
drunker still on freedom,
and I seduce her again.

Pandora's Box

Whoever made up that old story
about God being an omnipotent thing
didn't actually understand—or was in
denial—about the nature of man
and the peculiar god in whose image
he—but I'm not sure of the gender
here—was fashioned, this conflicted god,
a hunger for control in a universe set
into motion and then willed back
too late, this Pandora's Box of loneliness
and anger at a companion not his match,
his—or is it actually her—youth spent
playing the part of a god of wrath,
loathing herself all the while,
vowing to bring something called love
into the world when she cools off.

To Cain and Abel

Sit here, both of you, where you belong,
on the shelf attracting the dust you are,
housed with the family album of Jacob,
who wrestled each night with a sibling
angel, hoping to be beaten to a pulp,
imagining the promise of resurrection
by what he thought were perfect fists,
only to be smothered by jealous wings.

The scribbled tale of your blood feud
revealing so little of the true story
it might as well have been cremated,
packed into an urn for the three days
it took me to read the unopened letters
that passed for your correspondence.

Then it should have been poured
into a spring gale to feather away.

Esau without a Face

Who will know
poor Esau
without a face
now his brother stole fire

Who will remember his arms
muscled and burly
before the fruit
and milky porridge

Who will remember his voice
against the thief
the beloved
roasting the lamb

Who will remember him
crouching in
the empty
tent

Who will return to him
hands bearing
tender seared
meat

Salsify
    to Leo, who knows the salsify

I

Bloom of myrtle calls,
branches twisting praise
to a satisfied god.

II

An old woman's skin,
translucent as a baby's,
the quicksilver god.

III

A young woman's face
repudiating itself,
requiem for a god.

IV

Seed and syncope,
a pulse to germinate
the pulpy heart of god.

V

Salsify grows tall:
dandelions imitate
feather hands of god.

Piss on Saints

The charge stands
against soft guilt
dusting foreheads
with a smudged
cross of ash.

Against salt
rubbed on ulcers
already tender
with shame for
human sex.

Against manifestos
of happy martyrs
roasting like
piglets on a spit,
cut breast from rib,
Eve from Adam.

But especially
against stigmata
bleeding through
bandages hidden
by the doubting
sleeves of saints.

Reading Tarot

I worry over the card I've turned,
like it might be bad theology
to assign to an empty tree
the meaning of a man
pitched from a Tarot pack,
swinging from a limb.

And the ambiguity of it,
feet feathered to the ground,
not quite a broken neck,
his atheism still holding,
half dangling like a leaf
still tethered to its twig.

No answer swings here,
only half-strangled questions,
how one could want to leap
to flimsy faith from a firm edge,
how my hand could itch
toward the next card.

Heavy as a Wife's Body

>   *J.B.: He does not love. He Is.*
>   *Sarah: But we do. That's the wonder.*
>   Archibald MacLeish, *J. B.*

Job,
what color and texture is
the faith in your hands,
your desire for the Spirit
as heavy as a wife's body
daring you to forgive Him?

Shemuel,
what desire sculpted you
to nothing but a voiceless
praise, while tempting you
to choose the slick of human
dung over wide empty sky?

God,
what fleshy clones did
your bodiless breath
desire? In your earthly
hothouse these billions
still plead for the rapture.

Some Gods Don't Need Saints

The god who interrogates
conviction
has a body,
albeit one so dispersed
molecularly
that a tree could inhale
her soul
as if it were carbon dioxide
awaiting metamorphosis.

No matter her undelineated
shape,
she never suffers
the doubt
of true believers,
not even when mistaken
for the oxygen
that trees exhale
or the water flowing
from the faucet into the tub
that a local saint sits in
twice daily,
scrubbing breasts and arms
raw
to prove she hates
the texture of the skin
that traps her soul.

Some gods don't need saints
to feel real.

Martyr's End

You said it with embarrassment,
how you had tried for sainthood
and failed, no arrows in your side,
Saint Sebastian feeling your shame
and Jesus too because you didn't
know that nails are hammered
through the wrists, not the palms.

So I say to you "Oh, happy fall"
never to have slept on a bed
of river-dredged pebbles for a week,
never to have been so silly
as to pass up plump down pillows
for a bed of stone,
even red jasper or olivine jade
laced with warm minerals,
threaded with turquoise.

Oh happy failure, to lean into
a mountain climb, breathless
against its black quartzite,
its pink stippled boulders,
to crumble to a river bank
after a night of congress
with the twilight gneiss,
a rock great as God and just
as old, both having escaped
somebody's head
before the crushing
need for martyrdom was born.

Of Spiders

What stories would Grandmother Spider tell
if she knew
little brown spiders crawl
through holograms in museums,
if she knew
spiders crawl all over the internet
looking for choice bits of data to thief away,
if she knew
she has been tattooed on the backs
of raped women and gang members alike,
if she knew
I just pinched her fresh-hatched offspring
between forefinger and thumb
because they irritated my morning
coffee-brewing routine,
if she knew
nobody prays
to spiders anymore?

What would Grandmother say
knowing that cobweb stew
has not been on the menu
for at least thirteen centuries.

I admit it, I'd rather
bathe in patchouli-scented water
than dance like some old crone
naked and cold
around a dead willow tree
on the Winter Solstice.

Ts'its'tsi'nako

The weaver may measure your shroud,
the scissors of the three Fates snipping
the wormy silk of the mulberry tree.

Yet Creation is still the thread of a spider,
her legs plucking strings of the universe.

The angel may quiver into your chest,
a feather stirring the blood to a froth,
bringing the heart to the boiling point.

Still, rebellion makes a good lover,
Lucifer needing only a shared vision.

The trickster may slip into your bed,
Oden wooing with an elixir of youth,
a vial as precious to lovers as naïveté.

But belief still ferments in the marrow
of the bone, where fat can last forever.

Disabled Gods
of a painting by Van Gogh

The equilibrium of ice
and ember, crackle of
sleet pelting the blaze,
neither giving way to
the other, no question
of primacy, no competition
underwriting their dance,
no chance of drowning,
no third-degree burns,
their motion faithful to
the equipoise that keeps
our universe aglow,
its issue and return
a pattern for the seasons,
a guide to monthly moons
pushing water to and fro,
a template for the game
that ice and fire play.

Do you hear the trees
exhale as we breathe
in the clean winter air,
do you see the stone
turn itself outside in
before we break
apart the eggy geode?

In moments such as these,
and bigger still, in days
of living in a mob of bodies,
wall for wall, cage for cage,
blade for blade, I fall
toward the human myth
that rock and tree and sky
live for us, signs to guide
disabled gods ever poised
on thresholds of eternity.

But the breathing trees
live large and long,
the tides move to their
own song of sea and moon,
the stone enjoys a womb
of magma, birth by fire,
the issue and return of
these not bound to us
so much as we to them,
our lives a small contribution
to the universe that spiders
out its web of silk and dew.

Mary Catherine Harper is a poet and professor who organizes and reads poetry at the yearly SwampFire Retreat of artists and writers at *4 Corners Gallery* in Angola, Indiana, in collaboration with potter Steve Smith. Besides *Some Gods Don't Need Saints*, a semifinalist in the 2015 New Women's Voices Chapbook Competition, her poems have appeared in *The Comstock Review, Old Northwest Review, Cold Mountain Review, Pudding Magazine,* and *MidAmerica*. Her poem "Muddy World" won the 2013 Gwendolyn Brooks Poetry Prize of the Society for the Study of Midwestern Literature. See more about her interests at www.swampfire.org and www.mcharper.faculty.defiance.edu

www.ingramcontent.com/pod-product-compliance
Lightning Source LLC
Chambersburg PA
CBHW060227050426
42446CB00013B/3203